WARREN LEIGHT

Glimmer, Glimmer
and Shine

Grove Press
New York

Published simultaneously in Canada
Printed in the United States of America

FIRST EDITION

Library of Congress Cataloging-in-Publication Data
Leight, Warren
    Glimmer, glimmer and shine / by Warren Leight.
        p.   cm..
    ISBN 0-8021-3903-5
    1. Jazz musicians—Drama.   I. Title.
PS3562.E458 G58 2002
812'.54—dc2l   2001055746

Grove Press
841 Broadway
New York, NY 10003

02   03   04   05   10   9   8   7   6   5   4   3   2   1

For Donald and Edward

VERY SPECIAL THANKS:

Gordon Davidson
Nile Lanning
John McCormack

John Spencer
Evan Yionoulis

SPECIAL THANKS:

Allison Barcott
Terry Beaver
Sarah Bisman
Tom Bloom
Eric Bogosian
Joe Brancato
Johnny Carisi
Tony Campesi
Christian Casper
Joey Collins
Erica Daniels
Hope Davis
Ensemble Theatre of Cincinnati
Morgan Entrekin
Bridget Flanery
Jackson Gay
Maureen Grady Reed
Tim Guinee
Holly Harper
Beth Henley
Andrew Horn
Beth Klein
David Kolodner
George Lane
Don Leight
Edward Leight
Timmy Leight
The Long Wharf Theatre
Corinne Lucas

Evan Lurie
Manhattan Theatre Club
Steven Marcus
Mark Taper Forum
Andrew McCarthy
Ken McGee
D. Lynn Meyers
Jill Rachael Morris
Musso-Frank's Grill
The New Harmony Project
Dennis Parlato
Penguin Repertory
Eric Price
Kim Raver
Ilana Rose
John Ruocco
Kenneth Ryan
David Schwimmer
Ean Sheehy
Ron Taft
Larry Taub
Andrea "Spook" Testani
Ray Virta
Todd Weeks
Jeff Weiss
Williamstown Theatre Festival
Howard Williams and
  his Big Band
Emma Wilson

Author's Note for
Glimmer, Glimmer and Shine

I began by writing long monologues for Marty Glimmer. I had always known New York to be filled with Martins. Self-destructive, brilliant musicians (or writers or painters) who were too hip for the room in 1950. Forty years later, they were cobbling together a mix of cash gigs, music, copying jobs, an occasional big band arrangement or jingle chart, some teaching. And unemployment, always unemployment. They were barely hanging on to their rent-controlled apartments. Their health was past—their livers or hearts or lungs were betraying them. They were alone.

These guys, who had lived very full, often glamorous lives, found themselves marginalized. But boy could they talk. About the old days. About music. About McCarthyism and the Civil War and Lenny Bruce and baseball and Jim Crow and Crow Jim (the reverse racism of the jazz world) and Lord Buckley and Sherlock Holmes—all in one paragraph. They loved holding court, and I was often the only one around to listen.

Marty Glimmer was meant to be one of the sidemen in *Side Man,* but he didn't blend with the other guys. I finished *Side Man* without him. As time passed, more and more of the real-life Martys passed as well. They would die, and forty years of their stuff would be emptied out onto the street and poked through by passersby. Their own wives, siblings, and kids had long since lost touch with them.

After *Side Man* opened, I started to write about Marty again, and then about his estranged brother, Danny. The early draft was called *Glimmer Brothers,* until I realized I was writing not just about the brothers, but about their families (musical and professional). The jazz world I knew growing up was filled with or, rather, abandoned by, musicians who left the business and seemingly made good. I envied the stability their kids had known, yet was often surprised by how little they knew about their fathers and their fathers' history. *Glimmer Brothers* became *Glimmer, Glimmer and Shine,* a three-man trumpet section whose members' lives and families had traveled in very different directions. (The name came from a real-life one-night stand. In 1949 my dad, Don Leight, played in Buddy Rich's band alongside trumpet great Harry Edison. One night the masterful Bernie Glow subbed on the lead book. Glow, Leight and Edison never played together again, but musicians loved their luminescence.)

When *Glimmer, Glimmer and Shine* opened, I was surprised that some people thought I was siding with Marty and Jordan (the musicians) over Danny and Delia (the straight world). In writing the play, I gained an appreciation for the sacrifices made by both Marty *and* Danny Glimmer: Musicians who got hooked on jazz never had an easy ride. For those who *stayed in,* life was at best a roller coaster; for those who got out, a piece of them was left on the road. Marty may be the more charming and witty of the brothers, yet he is painfully aware of how far he is from being a hero or even a dedicated musician. The two men's families have also had to pay a price. Jordan Shine's parents overtly burdened his youth, but Delia too has been deprived. She may have grown up amid prosperity, but a central piece of her past has been withheld from her. In lieu of empathy, she was raised with a sense of entitlement.

The midcentury Martys and Dannys and Eddies are now all but gone. They were in many ways selfish men, yet they took better care of their music and their instruments than they did of themselves. Much of their music has been preserved. I wrote *Glimmer* in the hope that some of their stories, sacrifices and humor, would also be remembered.

FOREWORD

I had the privilege of directing *Glimmer, Glimmer and Shine* at the Mark Taper Forum in Los Angeles and for Manhattan Theatre Club in New York. It was a perfect bicoastal combination for a play whose present is set in Manhattan and Connecticut and whose past is 1950s Los Angeles.

We had two marvelous casts, with John Spencer playing Martin in both. And, of course, Warren was around sharing wonderful background on the world of the play and the characters—and working on the text.

I was attracted to the play's exploration of how the choices of one generation impact the next and how the avoidance of excess doesn't always lead to balance. It's a piece about a broken family whose members are forced to confront one another again and for the first time. There is wonderful comic energy but also a great deal of heart.

The play has its own music, a progression of duets and trios and Martin's wonderful solos. There are several scenes—the opening of the play, the first hospital scene where Delia and Jordan speak to each other while Martin in his coma speaks to us, and the scene where Daniel's visit pulls Martin back to consciousness—in which it was necessary to find just the right contrapuntal tension. These were the scenes on which Warren did the most textual work in Los Angeles. The one quartet at the top of Act Two was challenging in rehearsal but always played like gangbusters; it turned out that the audience's response was a key rhythmic line.

We started by educating ourselves in the literal music of the play, in the same way Jordan might be educating Delia (as well as seducing her) by giving her all those tapes. We listened to the Big Band pieces Martin, Daniel and Eddie would've played in their old days. We made sure everyone could tell the trombones from the trumpets and pick out the lead player's audacious line.

We listened to the later, cooler jazz, the "Brothers in Swing"–era music, through to the smaller and smaller jazz ensembles where no one hired a trombone anymore. And then to Jordan's music: sexy solo trombone and fabulously percussive Latin tunes.

We brought in pictures of Greenwich, Connecticut, and lavish weddings and some information on the garment industry. We found some great musician jokes like the one Martin taunts Jordan with in the first scene:

> What's the difference between trombone players and government bonds?
> *Government bonds eventually mature and earn money.*
>
> What do you say to a trombone player in a three-piece suit?
> *"Will the defendant please rise?"*
>
> What kind of calendar does a trombonist use for his gigs?
> *Year-at-a-glance.*

We even went to some hotel in Beverly Hills one Saturday night where there was a big band followed by a Latin band and took some salsa lessons in the lobby. We imagined what it would be like if the trombonist came down from the bandstand and tried to convince the actor playing Delia that her father had a twin and that he had studied with him.

The contrast between Daniel's new world and Martin's is, of course, so much one of economics. That contrast was made visible in the design of the play's two apartments, Martin's decrepit walk-up and Daniel's immaculate condo (impeccably rendered by set designer Neil Patel). We chose a twinning idea for the ground plans. Both contained a couch and coffee table and an upstage unit—a high-tech entertainment center for the condo and a pile of old boxes, records, magazines, cassette tapes and dirty coffee cups for Martin's. Each also had the same fifties-style chair (vintage for Martin's, retro chic for Daniel's), which we used in the restaurant scenes and the hospital.

At the Taper, with its three-quarter-round configuration, we had both apartments in place the whole time and played other locations center in front of them. At Manhattan Theatre Club's proscenium space, we could track the apartment furniture on and off and bring on other elements, such as a corner booth for the flashback scene at Musso's.

There were advantages and drawbacks to each solution. The Manhattan Theatre Club solution allowed for a cleaner look and less-crowded playing space in the non-apartment scenes, but the Taper's circular stage created some nice opportunities for actor movement. In the proscenium, one always knew the next piece of scenery was going to come on from either right or left.

For the end of the play, at the Taper, since both apartments were present, there was a nice overlap of Jordan's arrival into Martin's empty apartment and Martin's final exit from the condo. It was one of my favorite moments. In New York, it felt wrong to have Martin's apartment track on as he left the stage. Our solution was to pull the condo off-left as Martin disappeared up-right, leaving a lone chair floating in empty space as Jordan appeared. The bare space (beautifully lit by Donald Holder) made the loss palpable.

The musical centerpiece for our production was from an improvisatory session Warren's father and his fellow trumpeter Johnny Carisi had done a few years back for one of Warren's films. We played this glorious duet by two older trumpet players under Daniel's phone call to Martin. The composer, Evan Lurie, adapted one of the themes from that improvisation for the production's transitions and decided on solo trombone for the instrumentation. It was exactly right.

Of course, each production team will have its own journey with the play and make its own choices. I hope future collaborations will be as fulfilling and joyous as ours.

Evan Yionoulis
New Haven, 2002

ix

Glimmer, Glimmer and Shine was commissioned for a reading series by All Seasons Theater Company (John McCormack, artistic director). The world premiere of *Glimmer Brothers* (as it was then known) was originally produced by the Williamstown Theatre Festival (Michael Ritchie, producer). It was subsequently produced by the Penguin Repertory Company (Joe Brancato, artistic director, and Andrew M. Horn, executive director) in Stony Point, NY; and by Ensemble Theatre of Cincinnati (D. Lynn Meyers, artistic director).

Glimmer, Glimmer and Shine was originally produced in Los Angeles by Center Theatre Group/Mark Taper Forum (Gordon Davidson, artistic director/producer). It opened on January 25, 2001, with the following cast:

Delia	Alexa Fischer
Jordan	Jonathan Silverman
Martin	John Spencer
Daniel	Nicolas Surovy

It was directed by Evan Yionoulis; the set design was by Neil Patel; the costume design was by Candice Donnelly; the lighting design was by Donald Holder; the sound design was by Jon Gottlieb; the original music was by Evan Lurie; and the casting was by Amy Lieberman. The production stage manager was James T. McDermott, and the stage manager was David S. Franklin.

Glimmer, Glimmer and Shine was originally produced in New York City by the Manhattan Theatre Club, in association with the Mark Taper Forum. It opened on May 24, 2001, with the following cast:

Delia	Seana Kofoed
Jordan	Scott Cohen
Martin	John Spencer
Daniel	Brian Kerwin

It was directed by Evan Yionoulis; the set design was by Neil Patel; the costume design was by Candice Donnelly; the lighting design was by Donald Holder; the sound design was by Jon Gottlieb; the original music was by Evan Lurie; and the casting was by Nancy Piccione and David Caparelliotis. The production stage manager was Richard Hester, and the production manager was Michael R. Moody.

After its Ensemble Theatre of Cincinnati production, *Glimmer, Glimmer and Shine* was nominated for the American Theatre Critics/Steinberg New Play Award. After its New York City premiere, it was nominated for the Dramatists Guild's Hull-Warriner Award.

CHARACTER LIST

(Note: Six characters, four actors)

DELIA GLIMMER—female, mid twenties
The Greenwich, Connecticut, daughter of Daniel and Martha Glimmer. Upper-class, stylish (does marketing for her family's textile company), well-educated, intelligent; at times her cloistered upbringing makes her seem naive or condescending.

JORDAN SHINE—male, late twenties/early thirties
Bronx-born trombone player; caretaker/protégé of Martin Glimmer and others. Urban, sardonic son of trumpet player Eddie Shine; not nearly as self-destructive as his father's generation of musicians. Not yet living his life.

MARTIN (MARTY) GLIMMER—male, late fifties/early sixties
Gruff, funny, bitter, too-hip-for-the-room. Brilliant, but his own worst enemy: alcoholic, ex-junkie, now dying, but still filled with energy and anger. A talented trumpet player in the fifties, has cobbled together a meager, five-story–walk-up existence as a musician/teacher/arranger for forty years.

DANIEL (DANNY) GLIMMER—male, late fifties/early sixties
Martin's fraternal twin. In 1990: married, straitlaced, a successful, WASPy businessman, CEO of Glimmer Scarves; in 1955: a preternaturally gifted trumpet player and out-of-control junkie.

MARTHA GLIMMER (same actress as Delia)—female, mid twenties
Seen in a flashback (before she becomes the WASPY, successful Martha referred to throughout). During the fifties, a tough, cigarette-smoking, hard-drinking, jazz chick, caught in a

desperate situation. Working-class, on her own, the opposite of spoiled or prim.

EDDIE SHINE (same actor as Jordan)—male, late twenties
Darker, slicker than his son Jordan. Road-hardened trumpet player, boozer, ladies' man.

PLACE
The action takes place in Greenwich, Connecticut; various locations in Manhattan (Yorkville walk-up, VA hospital, high-floor condo, upscale restaurant); and Musso-Frank's Grill, L.A.

TIME
June 1990 through Autumn 1990.

ACT ONE

On one side of the stage, on a ratty couch, MARTIN GLIMMER *and* JORDAN SHINE *unwind . . . not that they were too wound up to begin with. Martin is a lifelong musician; Jordan is his protégé. He packs up his trombone.*

Downstage, find DELIA GLIMMER. *As she delivers her monologue she gradually transforms from a stylish woman with a sense of irony into a younger, less self-aware one; by monologue end she looks like someone drop-kicked from the pages of a Lands' End catalogue.*

She does not hear or notice Martin and Jordan. They do not acknowledge her.

DELIA I cannot tell you how it ends . . . I still don't know how it ends.

JORDAN (*To Martin*) I may have . . . met somebody.

MARTIN (*To Jordan*) "Somebody"? Can you be . . . a little more vague?

JORDAN (*To Martin*) Your niece, actually.

DELIA I *can* tell you it began innocently enough. At a wedding—

JORDAN (*To Martin*) It began *not* so innocently, at a wedding.

DELIA —thank God I wasn't asked to be a bridesmaid. It was 1990, the year when tout le monde, or at least every bridesmaid in Greenwich, had to wear that color; you know, not salmon, not peach, but *that* one—I always

I

looked a little carsick in it. Anyway. To the wedding: where I think I was The Only Single Person. Not *single* single, but Chuck was in Hong Kong—another takeover. And Mother and Dad were still on their buying trip, in India, (*Explaining*) for the company.

So . . . there I was, on my own for what felt like the first time ever. Which doesn't excuse, but maybe explains, why I had some, ohh, gaps in my emotional resume. The ceremony was High-WASP . . . a three-tenter: I forsake, you forsake, kiss kiss now can we drink? Amen and . . .

She crosses the stage. Back to the First Meeting. At a private club in Connecticut, 1990.

DELIA (*cont.*)   Over to the bar. And there is this swing band which, thank God, takes a break.

JORDAN (*To Martin*)   We finally take our break, not that anyone notices.

MARTIN (*To Jordan*)   I used to play gigs like that . . . with a transistor radio in my ear, listening to the ball game. Did they feed you?

DELIA   And I see one of the musicians (even in his tuxedo he looks like an orphan). He tries to order a drink. And the bartender says, "I'm sorry sir, we're not allowed to serve the help."

JORDAN   They're "not allowed to serve 'the help.'"

DELIA & JORDAN   "Rules of the club."

MARTIN   "The help?" Outstanding.

DELIA   So the musician backs away, like a townie at the 7-Eleven who's been carded. Just then, one of my dad's friends waves to me, "Ta-ta, Delia," and Boom!, bumps right into him. Gin spills all over his tux.

Jordan and Delia have moved toward center stage. Jordan reenacts the scene for Martin; Delia reenacts it for the audience.

JORDAN He spills gin all over my tux. Doesn't say anything. Just strolls away . . .

DELIA So I walk over to him . . .

She does—starts to hand him a napkin. The musician, Jordan, takes it from her.

DELIA *(To Jordan)* Here—

JORDAN *(Sarcastic)* Don't you just love Connecticut—the natives are *so* warm.

DELIA I grew up here, actually.

JORDAN Yes. Well. Did you? Start over. I'm Jordan Shine, trombone player.

MARTIN *(To Jordan)* Do you know the definition of a perpetual optimist?

JORDAN *(To Martin)* Yes.

MARTIN A trombone player . . .

MARTIN & JORDAN . . . with a beeper.

JORDAN *(To Martin)* Start over. *(To Delia)* . . . Trombone player. From New York. And I want to kill myself.

DELIA I'm sure you do.

JORDAN You're warming to me. Aren't you?

DELIA Not really.

3

JORDAN So, ah—what—it's Delia, right? Are you a friend of the bride, or the groom?

DELIA Yes.

JORDAN (*To Martin, exchanging a thumbs-up*) O-kayyy. (*Back to Delia*) And um . . . What do you do?

DELIA Marketing.

JORDAN Uh-huh. Could you be a . . . little more vague?

DELIA (*Begrudgingly*) For my family's textile company. Glimmer Scarves? I don't imagine you've heard of it.

JORDAN No.

She turns away from him.

JORDAN (*cont.*) But I know a Marty Glimmer, and his brother Danny.

DELIA My father's name is Daniel Glimmer.

JORDAN Danny Glimmer?

DELIA Daniel.

JORDAN Your dad's Danny Glimmer?

DELIA I really don't think it's the same one.

JORDAN No, wait a minute. You're Delia. Right? Delia Glimmer. That's right. And your mom is Martha. I'm Jordan Shine. Eddie's son.

DELIA Who?

JORDAN Eddie Shine. I'm Jordan! I used to study with your uncle Marty. Still do—(*To Martin*) sort of.

Delia has no idea what Jordan is talking about. He tries another prompt:

JORDAN (*cont.*)   Glimmer, Glimmer and Shine—the "Glow-in-the-Dark" trumpet section.

DELIA   I don't have an uncle.

MARTIN (*To Jordan*)   She's right. I don't have a brother. I have no kin at all. I've always been an orphan, since the day I was born.

JORDAN (*To Martin*)   Shh! (*To Delia*) Yes you do too have an uncle. Your father's twin. I mean, fraternal, but still—

DELIA   My father is *not* a twin.

JORDAN   He used to be . . . Oh c'mon, everybody knows the Glimmer boys. Especially Danny Glimmer. I mean, I don't *know* him know him—but I met him when I was a kid. I was with my dad, and we ran into him in the Village. (*Remembers this moment very clearly now*) He was taking his kid—that must've been you—to a matinee. Did you ever see *You're A Good Man, Charlie Brown* when you were like three?

DELIA   Didn't everybody?

JORDAN   My father said he was one of the greats—he and my old man roomed together on the road for I don't know how long it was—

DELIA   Has this approach ever worked for you?

JORDAN   Always. Listen: After Korea . . . (*Patiently now*) your father and *my* dad were touring with Johnny Carisi's band. Your father played lead—of course. My dad did the solos. They were on the road, a West Coast swing (*Snaps his fingers to jog his memory*) . . . L.A. I guess, yeah it had to be L.A. because that's when Quincy—Quincy Jones, you know who *that* is—

5

DELIA Isn't he married to Peggy Lipton?

MARTIN It'll never last.

JORDAN —he used to be a trumpet player. Anyway, short story long, he left the band in L.A. So they traded a saxophone player for your uncle, Marty Glimmer, who was with, I don't know—

MARTIN Mulligan—

JORDAN Mulligan . . . maybe. And that was it: Glimmer, Glimmer and Shine—the "Glow-in-the-Dark" trumpet section. 'Course, they didn't play together long, the band fell apart—

DELIA My father never played jazz.

JORDAN Well that *was* the rap on him. Truth is, he *could* solo, but everyone knew him for his lead playing—(*Sees she doesn't understand*) lead trumpet—(*Trying to explain*) like first violin. I guess. Lead trumpet sets all the phrasing the other horns follow—like those albums he did with Miles and Gil. He defined the whole sound of that band.

DELIA If you say so.

JORDAN I think I've even seen pictures of them—

DELIA (*Overlapping*) I believe you. OK?—

JORDAN —with my dad and your grandmother—

DELIA —You *think* you know my father. But—

JORDAN —in front of—

DELIA —it *can't* be . . .

JORDAN —the Glimmer Fabric Store. In the Bronx.

6

DELIA (*Surprised by the accuracy of this detail*) . . . the same person.

An awkward pause.

JORDAN Listen, here's my number. (*He pulls out a card; she backs up.*) Don't worry, it's for your dad. Do you see him a lot?

DELIA He's in India now.

JORDAN India? A lot of high-wage workers there? What do they get—like a rupee a scarf?

DELIA (*Defensive*) Mother handles the factories. He picks the fabrics. The workers *love* them. They always try to get jobs for their families—

JORDAN Whatever.

DELIA They do.

JORDAN Listen, when he gets back . . . tell him you met Eddie Shine's son. No: better—tell your dad you met his godson.

DELIA His what?

JORDAN I think he's my godfather—*there* was a swift choice on my parents' part . . . sorry. He wasn't . . . the most responsible guy in the world, like I'm telling you stuff you—

DELIA I think your group's getting ready to—

JORDAN Just tell your dad that Eddie's son, Jordan—that's me—met you at a party. Tell him Marty's doing better . . . that he's been basically clean for years—

DELIA (*No idea what he means*) Clean?

MARTIN (*With outrage*) Clean?

7

JORDAN (*To Martin*)   I mean, if you don't count half a bottle of scotch, a case of Diet Pepsi and three packs of Merits a day, yeah. (*To Delia as she exits*) He should give him a call.

Jordan rejoins Martin in his run-down, smoke-filled Yorkville tenement walk-up. Sunlight hasn't breached the studio in years. A downstairs buzzer rings.

MARTIN   Who's that?

JORDAN   Delia.

MARTIN   What!

Martin chain-smokes. Jordan desperately starts to clean up, or at least hide, the debris.

MARTIN   Are you, nuts? Bringing her here. The acorn does not fall far from the tree. The shit does not fall far from the weasel.

JORDAN   She wants to meet you. I think you should reserve judgment on—

MARTIN   Her mother is a weasel, Jordan. A social-climbing fart of a woman. She never met a back she didn't stab. A—

Apartment doorbell rings.

MARTIN (*cont.*) (*A manic riff*)   It's open. A . . . a dollar she wouldn't go down on and . . . *you* must be my niece Delia.

Delia enters the apartment. She tries to take it in. She is overwhelmed by the dirt, debris, and haze. She is dressed in a Connecticut country outfit, down to the black headband. And a little out of breath from the walk up.

MARTIN (*cont.*)   I was just reminiscing here with Jordan about your mom and dad. Don't be shv my dear, do come in. I'd get up, but the gout has got me by the balls. Don't be shy. You look nothing like your father, so aren't you the lucky one.

DELIA (*Overlapping with Martin below*)   Sorry I took so long, I thought there has to be an elevator somewhere but—

MARTIN   An elevator.

DELIA   —I couldn't find it—

MARTIN (*To Jordan*)   That's what this building needs—why didn't we think of it?

DELIA   —so I walked up the whole—

MARTIN (*To Delia*)   Find yourself a chair—

DELIA   —five flights it must have—

MARTIN   —it's over there under those underclothes.

Jordan races to clear the chair. Delia sits on the edge of the chair, tries not to let anything touch her.

DELIA   I'm a . . . I'm a—

MARTIN   Struggling to see the resemblance. Trying to imagine how someone such as me could be cut from the same cloth as yourself.

DELIA   No. Yes. Well. Actually . . .

MARTIN (*To Delia*)   Can you offer me a drink? Jordan, glasses all around. The cleaner ones are toward the top of the sink.

Jordan goes to offstage kitchen. Delia hands Martin a velvet gift bag; in it, a bottle she's brought with her.

MARTIN (*cont.*)   Chivas. Very nice—Jordan, how nice of you to tip her off. I used to drink it straight up, with a beer chaser. Then I got an ulcer so I mixed it with milk. Now I can't drink milk. I'm lactose-intolerant.

DELIA So's my dad. He had an ulcer too.

MARTIN He had more than that. So now I drink it with fermented soy milk or lactose-free milk. It's quite horrible once you get used to it.

DELIA Do you have any . . . iced tea?

JORDAN (*Returning with dismal jar/cups*) I don't think he does. Instant coffee.

DELIA Just water would be fine.

Jordan starts to go offstage for water.

MARTIN (*À la W. C. Fields*) Never touch the stuff myself. Fish fuck in it. Yes. Yes.

JORDAN (*Doubling back*) W. C. Fields.

DELIA Pardon?

JORDAN He's doing W. C. Fields.

MARTIN The comedian, not his brother, the department store.

JORDAN (*To Delia*) Marshall. Marshall Fields. Chicago store. No relation.

MARTIN Are you going to translate all evening?

Jordan, dismissed, goes offstage for water.

MARTIN (*cont.*) Now, young Delia, if you've come about your inheritance, I can assure you that I have provided for you in my will. Someday, as my sole niece, Chivas-bearer and, as of today, only speaking relative—all of this, all that you survey, shall be yours. How's Danny?

DELIA He's . . . he's . . . fine. You know him. Work, work, work. Oh, and he's trekking now. With Martha, in Nepal.

MARTIN Same old Danny. Except for the work, work, work part . . . and the *trekking*? Does he still have his chops?

DELIA Um . . . he doesn't eat meat.

Martin shoots Jordan a look.

JORDAN (*Handing Delia water*) Chops: jazz slang referring to lips, embouchure and more broadly, technical facility and musical ability on the instrument.

DELIA Oh, his chops. They're fine. I guess. A little chapped from running. He does marathons. Well, half marathons, now—

MARTIN Sure—he's my twin. Half for him, half for me.

DELIA Mother—Martha—doesn't think he—

MARTIN (*Coughs at the mention of Martha*) So he doesn't play anymore. Does he?

DELIA No . . . Never.

MARTIN What a shame. No matter what anyone ever said about your father, when he played, he was a motherfucker. He really was.

Delia looks to Jordan, who nods—it's a compliment.

DELIA Thank you.

Airport, night. (Note: The beginning of this scene should overlap with the end of the last. Overlaps, as much as possible, should be used between scenes. Delia should be pulled into Scene Two. Martin and Jordan can remain on their couch, listening to music in the dark, as Delia and Daniel play their scene. Transitions should seem fluid— like Martin's chain-smoking of one cigarette to the next.)

DANIEL Delia!

DANIEL GLIMMER, *scarf magnate, gets into the backseat of an airport limo. He and Delia "moi-moi" cheek-kiss hello. A trombone-led salsa combo plays on the car CD.*

DELIA Daddy! I was so worried.

DANIEL It was nothing.

DELIA Driver: We'll take the Merritt, not 95.

DANIEL Just the altitude.

DELIA How high were you?

DANIEL (*Reacts to this, then covers*) Oh . . . the altitude. Gets to some people more than others. Your mother was fine. I started to go a little . . . light-headed they call it. But the people running the trek—top-notch. They get on the satellite phone. Two, three hours later, Martha and I are being choppered back down the mountain.

DELIA Mother must have been a wreck.

DANIEL Happens all the time. After I stabilized, she wanted to cut the trip short. I told her, "Martha: Get back up that mountain." I figure, if she's up there, she can't shop.

DELIA (*Laughing at his joke*) Dad.

DANIEL Went back to the Rhiga, had a few meetings. It's all getting very modern over there—we may have to look around for a new country if it keeps up. Somewhere down the line. Malaysia—Penang maybe.

DELIA Vietnam?

DANIEL Who knows.

DELIA Dad, the oddest thing happened . . . I went to Maureen's wedding a couple of weeks ago—

DANIEL Hey, I almost forgot, I got you something.

Daniel pulls a small package from his jacket pocket.

DELIA —and I met this trombone player—

DANIEL *(Showing her)* They're Burmese rubies.

DELIA Oh, Dad (*Delia gives her father a "thank-you-for-the-gift" cheek-kiss. Note: This kiss is a well-worn family ritual.*), they're lovely. The thing is, he told me about his father, who—

DANIEL *Jesus,* what is this driver is listening to?

DELIA That's what I was trying to tell you, it's not the driver's. (*Turns up the volume on a remote control*) My friend gave it to me—

DANIEL Maureen?

DELIA No. The trombone player. He plays on it. And his father was a trumpet play—

DANIEL I don't want to hear it.

Daniel hits the stop-play button. Yawns.

DELIA Anyway, he launches into this story, at first I—

DANIEL Not now, I'm pretty wiped out . . .

13

DELIA But Dad—

DANIEL You can tell me all about it in the morning—

DELIA The thing is—

DANIEL Lights out, pumpkin. I am just crashing.

Delia looks down at her gift, then to Daniel.

SCENE THREE

Music up—same combo. Jordan and Martin in Martin's apartment. They pass a joint.

MARTIN Your generation ruined pot.

JORDAN We've been over this.

MARTIN My day, no one knew what it was. Danny, and *your* old man and I got high at Veterans Stadium.

JORDAN On the Fourth of July—

Now the next song on Jordan's tape, a more melodic, arranged piece, starts.

MARTIN Don't stop me if you heard the story—

JORDAN Against the Yankees—

MARTIN God, I hated them.

JORDAN Wait a minute. Veterans Stadium is a National League park.

MARTIN This is the problem with facts. I say: We were at the Vet, with eighty thousand people, watching the *Yankees*— God I really hated them—and we were getting high and no one knew what it was. But *you* guys had to go public with it.

(*Without missing a beat, now refers to the music they're listening to*)
Did you do this chart?

JORDAN   I took it from a head chart we'd been faking—I
wrote it down, fleshed it out.

MARTIN   It's good. Ballsy—nice voicings. Percussion sounds
like a train wreck.

JORDAN   It's hard to tone 'em down.

MARTIN   Break his hands. Shoot all the drummers. In my day,
we always had a chick singer—

JORDAN (*Has heard it before*)   . . . who was always making it
with the drummer.

MARTIN (*Ignores him*)   If he got his rocks off before the gig, he
wouldn't have to take it out on us during the gig. You
should get a chick singer. They always fall for the drummer.
(*Again, without a pause*) You hear from Delia?

JORDAN   We walked around the Village, went for a slice.
(*Pause for effect*) I made her a few tapes.

*Martin raises an eyebrow: Tapes are musician code for the first step in
seduction.*

JORDAN (*cont.*)   Some of my ballads. Miles and Gil. Carisi's
band.

MARTIN   She really doesn't know any of Danny's playing?

JORDAN   I think they listened to (*With disdain*) classical—

MARTIN   Jesus. That wife (*Starts to cough very hard*), if you'll
pardon the expression. She must have banned swing: Joseph
Stalin, Marshal Tito, Henry Ford and Martha Downs-
Glimmer.

JORDAN   I think Stalin may be a little over the—I mean, you haven't seen her in decades. How well can you—

MARTIN   My poor brother: a Connecticut Junkie in Queen Martha's Gulag.

JORDAN   How well can you know her?

MARTIN   Enough to loathe her. Imelda on dexies. Evita meets Synanon.

JORDAN   Reference?

MARTIN   California cult. Cleaned up junkies but made them stay in their retreats for the rest of their lives.

JORDAN   How strung out was he?

MARTIN   Not bad bad. Quart of vodka a day. Dexies at night. Junk. I mean, he could still get to a session—sometimes.

JORDAN   So she cleaned him up—

MARTIN   And cut his thing off. Sometimes, even when the disease is fatal, the cure is worse. She cut me out.

JORDAN   Maybe she thought you were a bad influence—

MARTIN   Bullshit—she *liked* bad influences. Besides, Danny was the—he hooked *me*. I wouldn't—the real reason she hated me—

JORDAN   Go on.

MARTIN   (*Hesitates, then comes clean*)   *Your* old man.

JORDAN   Eddie?

MARTIN   1955. L.A. I walked in on her and your father when Danny was stuck in New York. I never said word one about it to Danny. Or to her. Naturally, she never forgave me.

JORDAN   True story?

Martin is hit with a severe coughing jag.

MARTIN   What isn't when you get down to it?

He signals for a glass.

JORDAN   Water?

MARTIN   I would (*Coughs more*) but the (*Jordan hands him a glass; he drinks.*) fucking fish—

Scene Four

Delia, in a frenzy, crosses the stage to Jordan, who snuffs out a cigarette when he sees her approach.

DELIA   Jordan, sorry I'm late. Your city is one big gridlock. This creep was blocking the box and they never write tickets. And the parking . . .

They kiss.

DELIA (*cont.*)   Yech. (*Off his breath*) Jordan, you smoke?

JORDAN   It's a hobby. Listen—

DELIA   How's he doing?

JORDAN   He's fallen into a coma.

DELIA   What? I thought you—

JORDAN   His neighbors found him, collapsed, on the fourth-floor landing. EMS came and—(*Angry at himself*) I *told* him

17

I'd come by before our dinner, but he has to be stubborn. Went out to shop for himself—

DELIA   In this heat?

JORDAN   It wasn't just the heat. They think he's had a few silent heart attacks.

DELIA   Did the attending say that, or was this his cardiologist?

JORDAN   What?

DELIA   Where is his doctor?

JORDAN   He's more of a self-medicator.

DELIA   But—

JORDAN   Delia, not everyone has a doctor—

They go to the door of Martin's hospital room. Delia looks in and sees Martin.

DELIA   Oh my gosh. He's so pale.

Martin seemingly comes to.

MARTIN   Jordan!

Delia and Jordan do not react to Martin's voice.

DELIA   How long has he been like this?

MARTIN   Jordy!

JORDAN   (*To Delia*)   He was conscious when he got to emergency, but then they just left him on a gurney, and by the time I got here he was—

Martin gets out of his bed and speaks to the audience. Delia and Jordan cannot hear him. The rest of the scene plays out with Delia and Jordan talking to each other and Martin speaking to the audience.

MARTIN   I hate comas.

DELIA   It's not your fault . . .

MARTIN   I don't mind the needles, mind you. Anytime anyone brings a syringe near me, I perk up. Force of habit—no pun intended. But the rest of this . . . (*Looks at the bed, his robe, his visitors*) is beat.

JORDAN   Here's the other thing before he goes into the coma—

DELIA   He's going to be fine.

MARTIN   I listed Jordan as next of kin.

JORDAN   He listed me as next of kin.

DELIA   Well—that's sweet. You're like a son to him.

JORDAN   It's not sweet, Delia.

MARTIN   Sweet or not, the problem is, as soon as the nice people here at Our Lady of the Perpetual Invoice find out . . . as soon as they find out that he and I aren't related, they will not let him pull the plug. They may not even let him visit.

JORDAN   It's—they're going to ask me to make decisions that I don't want to make.

MARTIN   He's right.

DELIA   Oh—

JORDAN   It's not my—he and I never talked about—

MARTIN   And it's too bad . . . cause they're wheeling guys out of here in body bags like clockwork. Every five or six hours a lot of beeps and buzzes go off—a nurse rushes in. Then a doctor. Then they wheel 'em out.

DELIA   Well, I certainly don't think I should be making decisions like that.

MARTIN   The orderlies take book on which bed will kick first. These other guys, they don't look so good. So my money is on them.

JORDAN   Delia—not you.

MARTIN   If I lose,

JORDAN   His brother.

MARTIN   I lose.

DELIA   He was just sick himself; I don't know if—

JORDAN   I mean, I can't believe he still hasn't called Martin . . .

Delia doesn't say anything.

MARTIN   Uh-oh.

JORDAN   You didn't tell him yet. I thought you said—

DELIA   I've tried. He just—hits the stop button whenever I—

JORDAN   Jesus—what the hell is the deal with your family?

DELIA   There's nothing wrong with *my* family, thank you.

JORDAN   Nothing? Your mother bans jazz. She forbids all contact with your uncle 'cause she's afraid he'll rehook your father on dope. Your father goes along with it. He never even tells you you have an uncle. Then you don't tell your

father you met your uncle. Now you don't want to tell
your father his twin is—I thought my family was—

DELIA (*Crying*) Fuck you!

JORDAN Delia . . .

DELIA My father was never a junkie.

MARTIN Ha!

Delia and Jordan exit: Martin waits for them to leave.

MARTIN Ah—that Nembutal-Demerol cocktail is kicking
in—just like the old days . . . It's 1953 Ohio, Iowa—one of
those flat-ass Rodgers and Hammerstein states; you can give
me Hart over Hammerstein every time by the way . . .
Where was I? *Idaho*—and little Dickie Smith is enjoying
the hospitality of a woman whom we find out is the
mayor's daughter, and she's not really a woman yet, but
ever so slightly underage . . . and the mayor is of course the
town judge and police chief and hangman—and we're all
carrying our private pharmacies because it's a real viper
band, and these towns are not the easiest places to cop. And
the mayor, he starts to nose around our hotel and she's
inside, in Dickie's bed—or against the wall probably—
making noises.
   Making noises she doesn't want to lose her little Dickie:
She wants to go out on the road with us or some such
nonsense. And Dickie tells us about it on the bandstand.
   So that night me and Danny—he was never Daniel—set
it up so we burst into Dickie's hotel room with flashbulbs
popping like we're private detectives or reporters or FBI, for
crying out loud, and the chick is buck naked, and beautiful,
and she's lying there and Dickie pretends to be a hero—
which is pretty good for a guy who four-F'ed two wars—

and he hustles her into the bathroom and "negotiates" with us for the negatives and we leave. And then he tells her— "Honey, I bought our way out of this, but I don't trust those guys. We're gonna have to cool it for a while. I'll wire you when it's safe to join up with us"—and we leave town at four in the morning and we figure that's the last of it.

But by the time we get to the gig, Dickie's a basket case. Turns out he's nuts for the girl, so nuts he sends her a few of the pictures—like she'll want them for her scrapbook. Of course her father finds them, and that's why Dickie Smith had to stop touring and settle in California where he goes on to invent a food supplement for dogs. But to Dickie's credit, I could call him right now, if I wasn't in this coma, and he'd pick up with me like we were brothers.

And like a good brother *he'd* pull the goddamn plug. Because I have been sick before but this time I am certain I'm not coming back.

Martin gets back into his bed and retreats into his coma.

SCENE FIVE

In Connecticut. Daniel, fresh from a workout, makes a cocktail, sips it.

DANIEL   He had no right to drag you into this.

DELIA   Who?

Daniel doesn't respond—it's a technique of his.

DELIA (*cont.*)   Martin?

DANIEL   It's just like him—gets in a mess and expects someone else to clean it up.

DELIA   Dad, he's in a coma. He didn't drag me into this.

DANIEL   Oh yes he did. You do not know him like I do.

DELIA   Like a brother—

DANIEL   I do not understand why, if he was sick, if he'd had these silent . . . episodes—

DELIA   Heart attacks—

DANIEL   Whatever, why he didn't go into the hospital before he collapsed.

DELIA   Dad, maybe, if . . . you're not feeling well and you've been a junkie for half your life, maybe you don't want to know what—

DANIEL   (*Reacts to "junkie"*)   Junkie? Did this kid tell you that?

DELIA   Jordan? Well, not in so many—

DANIEL   What gives him the right to—

DELIA   Dad: That's just it, he doesn't have the right to— Martin listed him as next of kin. He isn't. He can't. You are.

DANIEL   No one would have known. He could have done what has to be done. But Martin—this is just what—if your—Do not mention this to Martha when she calls. Would you promise me that much? Please.

DELIA   When she calls? Isn't she back?

DANIEL   (*Vamping, as if covering something*)   She faxed this morning. From Bangkok—she is staying another week or so.

DELIA   I love how I find things out in this family. When were you going to tell me—

DANIEL There's a currency crisis in Thailand. The baht is absolutely worthless right now . . .

DELIA And. So?

DANIEL There may well be some . . . opportunities.

DELIA (*À la Jordan*) Could you be a little more vague—

DANIEL When does Chuck get back?

DELIA What?

DANIEL I don't think you would ever have talked to this boy—

DELIA Jordan.

DANIEL —if Chuck were here.

DELIA Give me a little credit.

DANIEL There is not much point in my visiting him. He cannot hear me. He can't—he's in a coma. Tell this kid—

DELIA Jordan. Your godson? Eddie Shine's—

DANIEL Tell him to use his judgment, and I will back him, sign off, whatever. He can fax me at the office.

DELIA This is your brother.

DANIEL I can't help that.

DELIA Dad!

DANIEL Look, I don't mean to sound harsh, but Martin is . . . irredeemable. Your grandmother tried with him, but he was hopeless—he'd only come around for a meal, or for a change of clothes or to borrow money—he had her completely conned, by the way—you know she paid his rent until he was forty?

DELIA How would I know? I didn't even know I had an uncle.

DANIEL I'm not going to defend what your mother did. Martin was—

DELIA Mother?

DANIEL —quite a charmer, in those days. But Martha, she— your mother *and* I, we both—look: This isn't about me. I don't care what happens to me; I could die tomorrow—

DELIA Dad . . .

DANIEL —but I've always wanted what was best for you. I wanted you safe, and healthy, and we had to make a decision, and I think it's clear. Look at you. You wouldn't be so . . . so—

DELIA (*Fishing for a compliment*) What?

DANIEL Untainted.

DELIA *Untainted.* Untainted?

DANIEL And fresh. And—

DELIA (*Pouring herself a drink*) You make me sound like a mineral water.

DANIEL Delia—Delia—nothing good comes from that crowd. That world—It's poison.

DELIA For me or for you?

DANIEL What?

DELIA Who was Mother protecting? Me or you?

DANIEL This discussion is closed!

DELIA (*Realizes she's pushed too far*) Dad—

DANIEL I said it's closed.

Daniel starts to walk out.

DELIA What about Martin?

DANIEL Tell you what—I will make some calls—

DELIA Thanks, Dad.

DANIEL But you have to promise me that you will stay away from this kid.

DELIA Dad, Jordan is just a friend.

DANIEL These guys. They cannot take care of themselves. And they certainly can't take care of someone else. All they know how to do is take. And I do not want that for you.

DELIA I'm still engaged to Chuck.

DANIEL Thank God for that.

DELIA We fax twice a day.

DANIEL Fine. You know what? I will remind Martha to look in on him.

DELIA Chuck's in Hong Kong, Dad. Not Bangkok.

DANIEL I don't see why everyone can't stay in Greenwich. It's not good to be on the road.

DELIA The firm promised him he'll be back by fall—he's working on a very big deal. He can't even say what it is.

DANIEL Fine. So then, there's no reason for either of us to be upset.

DELIA Fine.

Delia walks over to Jordan who has entered upstage. He hands her a cassette tape, she turns back downstage.

DELIA (*cont.*)   Oh—I almost forgot: I have something for you.

DANIEL   What is it?

DELIA   Jordan asked me to give you this. He said you'd recognize it.

Delia gives Daniel the cassette tape. No response. Delia walks back across stage.

DANIEL   *Brothers in Swing* . . . (*To himself*) Fuck.

SCENE SIX

Delia goes to Jordan in the condo. She begins to kiss him. Meanwhile, downstage, Daniel stares at the tape, then exits.

(*Note: The condo side of the stage is the mirror opposite of Martin's. It is a sleek, leather-and-glass, clean, cool, corporate pied-à-terre.*)

Delia and Jordan neck on the couch now as Jordan's trombone sounds on the state-of-the-art stereo.

DELIA   My father tried to warn me about you.

JORDAN   Remind me to thank him.

They kiss a little more.

DELIA (*Giggling*)   He doesn't really want me to get to know you.

Now Jordan pulls back.

JORDAN   Just wants me to fax him—like a what?—a sketch of a plug, and an outlet and a check next to: "*OK to pull*"? I

mean, your father is—sorry. Like I'm so much better. I
mean, here we are—Martin's in a coma, and we're necking.

Jordan turns off the music with the remote.

DELIA Why do you do that?

JORDAN What?

DELIA We were having a nice time.

JORDAN Very.

DELIA The rest of the world doesn't exist. And then you—

JORDAN Bring up reality—sorry. Bad habit. It's . . . an issue.
I'm supposed to be working on it.

DELIA You're not in therapy, are you?

JORDAN Just the last six years, or so.

DELIA You're joking.

JORDAN At least six. I'm much better than I used to be.
Haven't serial-killed anyone in weeks.

DELIA I've never been kissed by someone who's in therapy
before.

JORDAN Right. So how long have *you* been in therapy?

DELIA Me. Oh gosh, no. I mean . . . why? I'm fine.

JORDAN Oh.

DELIA I mean, really, therapy is for people with . . . serious
problems.

JORDAN I see.

He gets up, walks offstage to a kitchen.

DELIA No, I'm sorry. I didn't mean to . . .

JORDAN I'll get over it.

DELIA You can help yourself to anything—

JORDAN What kind of kitchen—(*Rummaging through a cabinet*) macadamia nuts, pistachios, Pepperidge Farm Mint Milanos—whose place is this?

DELIA Glimmer Scarves—we keep it for—if anyone is working late, or spending the weekend in the city or during Fashion Week.

JORDAN Kind of like a corporate fuck pad.

DELIA What?

JORDAN Never mind.

DELIA You do have a chip you know—

JORDAN Yes I know.

DELIA We could have gone to your place.

JORDAN Nooooo, I don't think that would have worked.

DELIA It's not in . . . Brooklyn is it?

JORDAN No.

DELIA Thank God.

JORDAN The Bronx.

DELIA You're kidding. I get it. Sometimes I can't tell with you.

JORDAN If I seem serious, I'm probably joking. If I joke about something, then it could be serious.

DELIA I've never understood the point of irony.

JORDAN Why *should* you.

DELIA So where do you live?

JORDAN The Bronx.

DELIA I didn't know there were nice parts of the Bronx.

JORDAN Sure—I don't live in them, but—

DELIA Is it like Martin's place?

JORDAN Cleaner. No open holes in the floor. And you can actually see through the windows. If you sit on the fire escape you can see the river.

DELIA That sounds lovely.

Moment of awkwardness, then:

JORDAN Here—

DELIA What?

JORDAN One of Martin's scrapbooks. He's always been very meticulous, for a pothead—although potheads are often surprisingly meticulous. The big picture gets cluttered, but little cut-and-paste jobs they can really get into.

She flips through the thirty-five-year-old scrapbook: photos of the Glimmer brothers, concert ads, Variety *reviews, itineraries.*

JORDAN (*cont.*) That's from *Metronome . . . Magazine*—'53, or '54—a review of the two of them, when they opened up the B-Sharp, on Fifty-second Street.

DELIA They owned a club?

JORDAN Them? No—just—first act to play it when it reopened, after you know—whatever marshal closed it for whatever.

30

DELIA The B-Sharp—I get it—the note, right?

JORDAN It's not really a true note—it's an alias; a B-sharp is a C.

DELIA Why?

JORDAN You never studied music?

DELIA No. Everything but. Mother made me take painting, and ballet. And tennis of course.

JORDAN Of course . . .

DELIA And ballroom and Français and—

JORDAN Not even piano lessons?

DELIA No. And they were actually de rigueur. She said I would just find it frustrating.

JORDAN Oh look . . . this is it—Carisi's band. Top row. Glimmer, Glimmer and Shine. The "Glow-in-the-Dark" trumpet section.

DELIA They're so . . . young.

JORDAN Everyone was young in those days.

DELIA Is that my dad?

JORDAN Let me see. (*Peers at the photo*) Danny's eyes are usually more closed than Martin's.

DELIA Oh, and he's got darker hair—

JORDAN Bad rug.

DELIA What?

JORDAN Toupe . . . Toupee?

DELIA My father would never wear a toupee.

JORDAN Probably has plugs by now. Sorry. Jordan Shine: denial buster. It's no big deal, those days they all wore rugs. Bandleaders didn't like a bald spot. In a sea of tuxes, it— (*Sees a photo . . . gets a little choked up*) Ohh, there's—

JORDAN (*cont.*) —my dad. **DELIA** —my mom.

They look at each other.

JORDAN (*cont.*) That's your mom?

DELIA That's your dad?

They look at each other, then at the photo. Slightly distance themselves from each other.

DELIA (*cont.*) How weird is that—(*Squints to read*) "Musso-Frank's Grill, L.A., 1955."

JORDAN Your mom was a babe. Look at her . . . dress.

DELIA Your dad was a handsome man . . .

JORDAN Sort of a lady-killer, according to my mom.

DELIA Do you think they're on a date?

JORDAN No! I mean—I don't think so.

DELIA That would be weird. Oh wait, they can't be. In '55 she and my dad were already engaged.

JORDAN There you go . . . (*Flips page*) Here's the whole rat pack. My dad, your dad, your mom—all they need's a bicycle and they'd have a bad French movie.

DELIA (*Doesn't get it*) What?

JORDAN Never mind.

DELIA Your dad had a *really* great head of hair.

JORDAN Rug.

DELIA Really?

JORDAN A lot of horn players were bald. Not the reeds, just the trumpets—

DELIA Come on—

JORDAN I'm serious; the union paper, *Allegro,* used to have ads for Chinese restaurants, cheap tuxes and toupees. Discounts for trumpet players. Even *my* hair started to fall out when I was sixteen. That's why I switched to trombone.

DELIA Sixteen?

JORDAN Right after my father died. Handfuls of it.

DELIA That could be stress-related.

JORDAN I think it's genetic.

Jordan closes the scrapbook, withdraws.

DELIA Poor Jordan—the world on your shoulders.

She massages his shoulders. He enjoys it.

JORDAN You've got strong hands.

DELIA Tennis.

JORDAN You would have been a good piano player.

Jordan hits the remote control; the romantic trombone returns. They resume kissing.

The hospital. Martin, out of his bed, but still in his coma, begins a monologue.

MARTIN   So I'm going through this tunnel—something like the Midtown Tunnel, only: no cars, the tile on the walls is Mexican, and I got the whole tube to myself. And I see this shaft of light at the end, and I'm thinking: This is it, it's *that* tunnel, the golden light. I'm graduating. The big mystery is about to be unveiled to me. I'm wondering, Will there be music? Will I like anyone? Do you have to dress for dinner? And now I'm not even walking—I'm just moving; there is no gravity and I am gliding through the air; jump time.

I look down at my body, and I'm reed-thin, like the teenager I never was—and I'm just in flight. Nothing hurts. First time in forty years—no pain. My lungs are clear, my face is smooth; my hair is moist from ocean mist.

Daniel walks into Martin's room. He goes to Martin's bedside. He plays his scene to the bedside as if Martin were lying in the bed, deep in his coma.

DANIEL   Martin. It's me. Daniel—

Martin does not see or react to Daniel. He does, however, interpolate Daniel into his fever dream . . .

MARTIN   I think I hear a foghorn—

DANIEL   —your better half.

MARTIN   —or a train whistle in the night—E, E-flat—

DANIEL   God, what happened to you?

MARTIN   —but then it sounds again—

DANIEL   Can you hear me, Martin?

MARTIN —and I realize it's someone calling my name.

DANIEL I can't believe we haven't—

MARTIN It's coming from behind me, from Alcatraz.

DANIEL It's been so long.

MARTIN So I start trying to really book because I know only one thing and that is—

DANIEL I should have come earlier.

MARTIN I DO NOT WANT TO GO BACK.

DANIEL (*Looks at his brother, gets no reaction*) I don't know if you can hear me, but if you can . . .

MARTIN No one's home. Go away.

DANIEL I got ahold of the wildest cassette the other day—dig this: *Brothers in Swing*.

MARTIN And now, I start to hear music—it's me, playing like I did forty years ago.

Daniel and Martin listen in their own worlds to the two trumpets trading four-bar solos.

DANIEL & MARTIN I guess we could really blow back then.

DANIEL When we're trading fours—even *I* have a hard time knowing which one of us is which.

MARTIN —but I don't care. Because I am by now only a few dozen yards from the opening. And beyond it, a meadow by the water. I can smell the air and it is so sweet and warm and I swear I hear children playing, and birds singing, and then my *fucking* name gets called again.

DANIEL Martin—

35

MARTIN God I hate my name.

DANIEL I—

MARTIN Never liked it, so I ignore it.

DANIEL Martin, please . . .

Daniel simulates grabbing and holding Martin's hand. Martin returns to the foot of his bed, slowly starts to climb into the bed and fall back into his coma.

MARTIN Now, from out of the fog—something *grabs* hold of me. From behind. A hand grabs my wrist and I wish my hand would come off my arm like meat off a drumstick but instead there's this rifle recoil: CRACK! And the tunnel seals off in front of me and I'm gasping for air. My lungs are old again. And scarred. And my bridgework starts to hurt and my tracks reappear; my abscesses burn and the fungus is back up under my toenails and I look up and I see . . .

DANIEL Martin!

The two worlds, Martin's fever dream and Daniel's bedside vigil, connect. Daniel holds a comatose Martin's hand. And Martin starts to come out of his coma. He looks up and sees Daniel. The next several lines overlap.

DANIEL (*cont.*) Martin? Martin. You're OK. It's OK. I'm here. You're back!

MARTIN No, I'm gone. I'm walking down a road . . .

Martin tries to leave the bed—he's not all the way back to reality. Daniel tries to hold him down.

DANIEL You're in the hospital.

MARTIN It's lined with Asian hookers—like a casting call for Miss Saigon—

DANIEL Calm down.

MARTIN —and I'm walking toward this neon light, the golden-red neon of a Third World bordello. And it's blinking:

DANIEL Martin.

MARTIN Mar-Tin.

DANIEL Martin.

MARTIN Mar-Tin. (*At last makes full eye contact with Daniel and reality, and jumps back*) Ahhh!

DANIEL Ahhh! Take it easy. Take it easy.

MARTIN (*Comes to, sees him*) The girls were kissing on me, and putting garlands of fruit and reefer around my neck and then just as I was about to—

DANIEL I'm going to call the nurse.

MARTIN (*Coughing*)—you called me back you schmuck and it all sealed up. *What in God's name are you doing here?*

They now take each other in, fully, for the first time in thirty-five years.

DANIEL I'm your brother . . .

MARTIN I'm in purgatory; there's been a glitch.

DANIEL I would have been here sooner, but—

MARTIN You didn't know I was alive, Danny, how could you know that I was dying?

DANIEL It's Daniel.

MARTIN Whoever you are, I didn't even want you to know I was here.

DANIEL They wanted me to sign some papers—

MARTIN I listed Eddie Shine's kid as next of kin.

DANIEL —but I thought I should see you first. It's a good thing I came when I did.

MARTIN Your timing was bad—

DANIEL No—it was good. My being here probably helped you come out of it.

MARTIN Ahh—but a few minutes earlier you'd have seen the nurse.

DANIEL Was she cute?

MARTIN She had Demerol, Daniel. Enough for the three of us.

Across stage, EDDIE SHINE, *played by Jordan, appears in a fifties suit, and haze . . .*

DANIEL (*Walking out*) Martin.

MARTIN You, me and Eddie Shine . . .

Martin now watches from his bed as Eddie Shine appears onstage, in 1955 . . .

SCENE EIGHT

Musso-Frank's. 1955. It's a classic red banquette L.A. Italian joint. Eddie and MARTHA GLIMMER, *played by the actors who play Jordan and Delia, are about to toast. They are dressed from another era—Martha wears a very sexy dress, Eddie a great fifties suit; his hair is slicked back. Jazz cocktail piano underscores the entire scene. (Note: Eddie is a far tougher guy than his son, Jordan. Martha, who may have become a Connecticut businesswoman, did not start out that way. In 1955 she was a cool jazz chick, in a desperate situation.)*

Downstage, out of his bed, Martin watches the entire following scene unfold. Eddie and Martha are unaware of his presence.

MARTHA Eddie—

EDDIE Martha, you made it.

MARTHA Threw somethin' on and came right here.

EDDIE You clean up good.

MARTHA You wanna mess me up?

She kisses him, passionately.

EDDIE I take it we're solo.

MARTHA We are. Danny's a scratch.

EDDIE (*Toasting*) To . . . clandestiny.

MARTHA To us.

They interlock their arms, sip and kiss.

EDDIE God Martha. It kills me when I see you, but I can't be with you.

MARTHA I know. It drives me crazy. Which is why—

They overlap their next several lines.

EDDIE Then why can't we—

MARTHA —I thought it might be a—

EDDIE —change the rules?

Martha stops, not sure if she heard this or made it up.

MARTHA What?

Another pause. Eddie backs up.

EDDIE You first.

MARTHA But—

EDDIE Don't worry, Martha, you'll still get the last word.

MARTHA I've been thinking . . .

EDDIE Uh-oh.

MARTHA Can't we just stay here, Eddie? Forever?

EDDIE I think they're getting ready to close. L.A. folds up by nine. Not that there's much to fold.

MARTHA No I mean, *stay*. Stay.

EDDIE In L.A.?

MARTHA When the bus goes, we stay . . . The two of us.

EDDIE What would we do at night?

MARTHA (*Flirty*) We'd think of something.

EDDIE There's, like, two clubs to play. Maybe three. Half the guys here are moving to Vegas—

MARTHA Vegas? That's no place for kids.

EDDIE Now *there's* a worry I don't—

He stops. She lifts her glass again.

MARTHA To us.

EDDIE (*Finishes his drink*) Am I following you—

MARTHA I'm just saying—if we *were* going to settle down, Las Vegas wouldn't—

EDDIE (*Unsettled now*) Baby, you're crazy, and I'm crazy for you but—settle down? Settle down and do what?

MARTHA Dickie Smith's got a business going.

EDDIE Dog food?

MARTHA It could be anything.

EDDIE What?

MARTHA (*Looks around*) Hats. Dishware. Just not jazz.

EDDIE You want me to give up playing now.

MARTHA You could still *play* . . . you can, you can sit in with your friends, on weekends. Or teach . . .

EDDIE So, it's like that? (*Thinks it through*) I bet it's not even my kid. You want me to give up the business, and it's Danny's kid. Not mine, right?

MARTHA (*Coming clean*) Fielder's choice.

EDDIE So, Danny already said no?

MARTHA He called to say he was hung up in New York for another week. I thought, before I told him, you and I could get a little time to ourselves *finally,* to—we've never had the chance to—

EDDIE Those were *your* rules, Martha. Danny plays lead; I hold his chair when he's away.

MARTHA Or passed out. He's making some mess of his life. Half the time he's so stoned he—

EDDIE Hey—give the guy a break. You're talking about my best friend, and your fiancé.

MARTHA The funny thing is, you and I get on so much better.

41

EDDIE   We have more in common.

She leans in and tries to reconnect to him.

MARTHA   We do?

EDDIE   We both take care of Danny.

Suddenly an unseen "souvenir photographer" approaches them.

EDDIE *(cont.)*   Hey—

Too late. A photo flash goes off.

EDDIE *(cont.)* (*To the unseen photographer*)   Who the hell told you we wanted a photo?

MARTIN   I did.

Neither of them hears him.

MARTHA   Eddie, listen—we make a good team.

Now, Eddie sees someone, downstage. Freezes.

EDDIE   Oh Jesus.

MARTHA   A real good team—

EDDIE (*Sotto voce*)   Guess who's standing at the bar. Staring at us.

MARTHA   Not Danny?

EDDIE   Close.

MARTHA (*She turns downstage to see*)   Martin.

Eddie gets up, as if he were about to flatten Martin.

EDDIE   What the hell is he doing in L.A.?

Martha stops him.

MARTHA   Eddie, please—cool it.

Eddie stops in his tracks.

MARTIN   (*A pledge to himself*)   I won't say a word.

MARTHA   (*To Eddie*)   We don't say a word.

END ACT ONE

ACT TWO

Back at the hospital. Martin is looking a little better. He sits up, eats Jell-O from a tray. Watches TV as Daniel enters.

DANIEL Martin? Martin. They've got you in *here* now?

MARTIN You're back? . . . Third time's the charm.

DANIEL Your name wasn't on the door. At intensive care. I got worried.

MARTIN How do you think *I* felt when I saw that? They moved me. To minimum security.

DANIEL They should tell people. Me. I'm next of kin . . . I was worried. Wandered around the hospital—no one knew anything. No one knew. I was very worried.

MARTIN Apparently they put me on a new drug, and I responded. *There's* a shock. Hey—you want some Jell-O?

DANIEL Nah—

MARTIN Cold turkey?

DANIEL Martin, enough with the cheap shots.

MARTIN (*Lifts the lid over his dinner*) No, I'm asking you if you would like some cold turkey. Every meal's an adventure here.

DANIEL I had a bitch of a time figuring out what to do with the car. It's Friday night; the town is packed.

MARTIN Friday, is it? What year?

44

Daniel is busy staring out the window.

DANIEL   And all the garages around here are underground.

Martin starts to have a coughing fit.

MARTIN   (*He cannot stop coughing*)   Pass me a ... pass me a—

DANIEL   Water?

MARTIN   (*Still coughing*)   —cigarette.

DANIEL   Where are they?

MARTIN   Yours. The bastards don't let me have 'em. (*Coughs more*) One of yours.

DANIEL   I quit. Years ago. Don't even miss 'em now.

MARTIN   That's great.

DANIEL   Can you believe it?

MARTIN   No.

DANIEL   Where was I—

MARTIN   You were about to leave.

DANIEL   No. (*Remembers*) The car.

MARTIN   Of course. The car ... You know, if the car makes you so nervous, maybe you should take the train.

DANIEL   The *train*? It's taken care of. I found this doctor's lot, in the courtyard. MD plates only. But I slipped the kid twenty bucks to keep my car just at the gate, and I told him there's twenty more when I get back.

MARTIN   (*Gravel-voiced, à la Joe E. Louis*)   "Nobody ever went broke from tipping."

DANIEL   (*Recognizing the bit*)   Joe E. Louis ...

45

MARTIN The comedian. Not his brother, the singer.

DANIEL Martin?

MARTIN & DANIEL Martin and Lewis.

MARTIN Remember that tour?

Martin now shrugs his shoulders, indicating "laughter."

DANIEL That's right, Jerry always wanted everyone to think he was cracking up the band. So we had to—

They both now laugh/shrug in unison.

MARTIN Whether that imbecile was funny or not.

One more shared shrug.

DANIEL Martin and Lewis . . . God.

As the reverie fades . . .

MARTIN They broke up too, you know.

DANIEL This place is a . . . a real pit. You know, I have—I know this cardiologist, he's top-notch; maybe he could come . . . (*Looks at the dilapidated ward*) Maybe you could go . . . How long do they think they'll keep you here?

MARTIN They want me out; I'm just in a Thomas Wolfe situation.

DANIEL What did he have?

MARTIN I can't go home again.

DANIEL What are you afraid of?

MARTIN The six-story walk-up.

DANIEL You are not still in Yorkville?

MARTIN (*Proud*) Just like the old days—except forty more years of stuff. Once it goes up six flights and in, it never comes out.

DANIEL You are not still there?

MARTIN I still have your couch. That plaid one.

DANIEL I never had a plaid couch.

MARTIN Those who would forget the past are condemned to reupholster it . . .

DANIEL How long can you stay here?

MARTIN The social worker's trying to get my Medicaid reinstated.

DANIEL Reinstated?

MARTIN You're eligible as long as you're in a coma, but when you come out of it, you're fucked. It screws up their paperwork.

DANIEL Jesus. This fucking city.

MARTIN It's federal Daniel.

DANIEL You are not thinking of staying with us, are y—

MARTIN I don't do well on Greenwich *Mean* Time.

DANIEL Is there anyone else who—

MARTIN I'm not a good roommate, remember?

DELIA Why doesn't he stay at the condo?

DANIEL (*Turns to see*) Delia?

DELIA Hi Dad. This is Jordan. Your godson.

Jordan puts out his hand. Daniel is at first taken aback by Jordan's resemblance to the young Eddie. But he stays on point.

47

JORDAN Nice to meet you—although, actually, we met once when I was a kid.

DANIEL Did we? (*Cuts him out*) The condo's not really set up for—it's really for business. (*To Martin*) The company. Clients.

DELIA The trade show isn't for months—

MARTIN What are we talking about?

DELIA Glimmer Scarves has a pied-à-terre in midtown.

JORDAN It's great! It's got an elevator and a Jacu—

Daniel shoots Delia a dagger for having taken Jordan there.

JORDAN (*cont.*) I helped Delia carry some . . . ah . . . plants.

DELIA (*To Jordan, pissed at his bad bluff*) Plants?

MARTIN (*Distracting them*) An elevator—imagine that.

DANIEL It's not going to work—there are rules, you know.

JORDAN Well, the social worker said as long as he doesn't own it, it won't count against his Medicaid spend-down.

MARTIN I think Dan means Martha's rules.

DELIA She's away.

JORDAN Still?

DANIEL (*Hurriedly*) Traveling for the company. Thailand. The baht. Just been *tumbling*—

MARTIN Tell me about it.

DELIA We should do it before she gets back. That way it's a fait accompli.

MARTIN A Greek cheese?

JORDAN When is she due back?

DELIA & DANIEL She's—

DANIEL —out . . . buying. For the company. Fifteen-hour days.

MARTIN She's a saint. You married a fucking—

DANIEL Don't you dare, Martin—

MARTIN —saint, Danny.

DANIEL It's Daniel.

MARTIN Fielder's choice.

DANIEL I beg your pardon.

MARTIN Not hard enough.

DANIEL (*To Martin*) I wouldn't push your luck if you want our charity.

MARTIN *Charity?*

DANIEL What would you call it?

MARTIN Look, you can take your fucking tax shelter—

JORDAN (*Overlapping with Martin*) All right, Martin, Martin, stop it!

MARTIN It's not me! It's him!

JORDAN BOTH OF YOU! Time-out.

DANIEL (*Pushing Jordan away*) Stay out of this, Eddie.

JORDAN Eddie—?

MARTIN It's Jordan!

DANIEL Whoever the fuck you are!

MARTIN And I'd rather stay here and cough up phlegm and—

DANIEL (*Overlapping with Martin and Jordan below*) Fine. Suit yourself then, stay here . . . stay here and rot for . . .

Daniel and Martin seem ready to fight.

JORDAN (*To Daniel, protecting Martin*) WHAT THE HELL ARE YOU DOING?

MARTIN —eat yellow food than take your crust of bread. So don't—

DELIA Stop it!

JORDAN Martin—

DELIA Stop it!

JORDAN (*Overlapping ends*) Do you get it? You can't stay here!

DELIA All of you. Jesus.

JORDAN This isn't a joke.

MARTIN NO. You're right. The joke would be: What does Martin have in common with a drummer who breaks up with his girlfriend?

JORDAN (*Not amused*) Very funny.

DELIA (*Re: the whole situation*) I give up.

JORDAN & DANIEL They're both homeless.

DELIA I don't get this.

MARTIN The joke's on me.

DELIA You're not homeless. We have a perfectly good *empty* condo—

DANIEL I'd have to speak with my accountant—

MARTIN Me too.

DELIA Dad—

DANIEL That condo is for—it's not a good long-term solution.

DELIA Short-term though, it's perfect. There's even a gym in the building, for his physical therapy.

MARTIN Oh bully.

JORDAN Martin—

DANIEL You have obviously thought this all out, Delia—

DELIA Do you have a better plan?

DANIEL So, what do we tell your mother?

DELIA Since when does anyone in this family tell anybody anything.

She walks out. Jordan follows.

MARTIN (*To Daniel*) I don't know where she gets it from, Daniel. I really don't.

Martin turns the volume back up on the TV. Eats his Jell-O.

SCENE TWO

Restaurant. Night.

JORDAN So—the hospital's so happy to get him out, they even got God knows which agency to spring for a visiting nurse.

DELIA I'm really impressed with the way you deal with all this.

JORDAN Years of training. And I'd still be battling the VA if you hadn't—

DELIA I got you something.

She hands him a small package.

JORDAN For what?

DELIA I just think—you deserve something for . . . taking care of my uncle.

The gift sits between them.

DELIA *(cont.)* Aren't you going to open it?

JORDAN I don't like gifts.

DELIA Jordan—

JORDAN I'm not good at opening these. OK., OK.

He opens it with no respect for the lovely wrapping job. He stares at:

JORDAN *(cont.)* A *belt?*

DELIA That one you have is kind of . . .

JORDAN What's wrong with my belt?

DELIA You could use a new one.

JORDAN Um, thanks.

She leans in. He looks at her. Realizes he is supposed to kiss her cheek. He does.

JORDAN *(cont.)* I told you—I'm lousy at this. Gifts always depress me.

DELIA You're going to have to get over that.

They go silent for a moment.

DELIA *(cont.)* I don't "get" this whole "depression" thing.

JORDAN You don't *get* it?

DELIA I mean, if you're in a bad mood, change the station.

JORDAN It's not that easy.

DELIA What about your therapist? What does he say?

JORDAN *She* says, I'm depressed. And we need to work on it.

DELIA Oh—well, "Ask the barber if you need a haircut."

JORDAN What does *that* mean?

DELIA Nothing. What's your shirt size?

JORDAN I have plenty of shirts.

DELIA Are they all plaid?

JORDAN I don't know. Who pays attention to clothes?

DELIA Everyone.

JORDAN Can we change the station?

DELIA I mean, the way you look is important. Granted, it's only an image, but people judge you—like your hair—

JORDAN What's wrong with my hair?

DELIA Have you looked at it lately?

JORDAN (*Tries to look at it*) No.

DELIA Really?

JORDAN I can go weeks without looking in a mirror. Every once in a while I walk by one and I go—Jesus, what happened to that guy? Then I get my hair cut.

DELIA You sell yourself short.

JORDAN I don't sell myself at all.

DELIA I could, Jordan.

JORDAN What?

DELIA Sell you. Introduce you to people. Walk you around. The Erteguns, Ahmet and Mica, have a cottage near us. The—

JORDAN Delia—

DELIA You're undervalued.

JORDAN I play trombone, Delia.

DELIA Didn't you tell me Quincy James used to play trumpet?

JORDAN Jones. Quincy Jones, and what does he—

DELIA But I look at you and I see—it's like when you see a company that's been battered down for a long, long time. A stock that's been hammered. I know, I know—who wants to catch a falling knife? But I think this company has value.

Across the stage, Martin, in hospital clothes, enters, with a walker. He tries to make sense of what Delia says.

DELIA (*cont; to Jordan*)   Underlying assets. And if someone could come along and unlock those assets, well that stock, that stock is going to double and split and double again.

JORDAN   I have *no* idea what you are talking about.

DELIA   I'm talking about you, Jordan.

MARTIN (*To Jordan*)   You're a stock now?

JORDAN (*To Martin*)   A depressed one, with upside potential.

Jordan and Delia stay seated. She is still at dinner. Jordan is both at dinner and recounting the dinner to Martin.

MARTIN   Is that her idea of hot talk?

JORDAN   She said I could be the next Quincy James.

MARTIN   *I* didn't think we needed the first one.

JORDAN   You all set for tomorrow?

Jordan keeps his focus on Delia, while talking to Martin.

MARTIN   My honorable discharge? I packed my urine bottle . . . as a souvenir and flower vase.

JORDAN   Lovely.

MARTIN   Most of the stuff I need is up at my place . . . I never know what to pack for a coma. And then, by the time I come out of it, I'm completely wrong for the new season.

JORDAN   I'll try and get Daniel to drive in and meet me at your place.

MARTIN   He'll need an armed guard for the car. Is this . . . condo, an office? Or a—

JORDAN   It's like a Mariott Marquis de Sade wet dream. Leather and . . . leather and . . . more leather in the living room; polished granite in the kitchen—

MARTIN   There's a kitchen?

JORDAN   More than that. There's a minibar. Macadamia nuts—wall-to-wall.

MARTIN   Minibar? So why do you two lovebirds always go to restaurants?

JORDAN   So I can get humiliated when the check comes.

Delia hands him the check. He smiles at her. Jordan now turns to Martin.

JORDAN *(cont; to Martin)*   Guess how much it cost.

MARTIN   Tonight? In that shirt? . . . Eighteen dollars—

Jordan shakes his head.

MARTIN *(cont.)*   More? *(Jordan nods)* Fifty? A hundred?

JORDAN   Keep going.

MARTIN   I can't. I'm on blood thinners. I'll get dizzy.

JORDAN   One eighty-nine. One eighty-nine. I said, *(Turns to Delia, and nonchalantly asks)* How did you choose this place?

DELIA *(To Jordan)*   I like the lighting.

MARTIN *(To Jordan)*   Well, you didn't tell me it was well lit.

JORDAN   And then I figure, my therapist would want me to say something, set a *boundary,* because you know—it was lucky I had enough room on my Visa to take the hit.

MARTIN   Bad move.

JORDAN Paying for it, or saying something?

MARTIN All of the above.

JORDAN So I very, very, sweetly say how much I like the restaurant—but: (*To Delia, at their table*) Just so you know, Delia, I can't do this all the time. I mean I had a nice meal, my . . . couscous was terrific—but unless it's a special occasion—like a *really* special occasion—(*To Martin*) like an occasion so special I can't even imagine it—(*To Delia*) I'm not comfortable spending one eighty-nine plus tip on dinner for two on a Tuesday night.

Martin walks over to the restaurant now.

MARTIN Uh-oh.

JORDAN So she sits there for a second, doesn't say anything, and when we walk out on the street, she starts to cry.

Delia gets up, upset. Walks out. Martin takes her seat at the table. Jordan sneaks him a cigarette.

MARTIN What's with the Glimmers all of a sudden? Tears are raining down like . . . like rain.

JORDAN We're walking through the Village and everyone's looking at her crying, and then they look at me like, "What did you do to her, you bastard?"

MARTIN You told her you didn't love her. Of course she's going to cry.

JORDAN What?

MARTIN Spending money. That's how she knows someone loves her. If he buys her things. Scarves. Jewelry. Dinner. Doesn't matter what—as long as it's expensive. That's how you express affection in Greenwich. Margaret Mead did a whole special on it.

JORDAN That sucks.

MARTIN Did she give *you* anything?

JORDAN She got me this belt. And she said something about buying me shirts, or shoes and—

MARTIN No further questions at this time.

SCENE THREE

Daniel and Jordan are at Martin's apartment, putting things in bags to take to the condo. Daniel uses a handkerchief to touch things.

DANIEL How does he live like this?

JORDAN I don't think he sees it anymore.

DANIEL Even the clothes *in* the bureau are dirty.

JORDAN (*Protective*) He gets behind when he's not feeling well. (*Daniel looks out the window.*) Your car should be fine. (*After a moment*) You know that album the two of you did, *Brothers in Swing*?

DANIEL Tough session. The engineer was a train wreck.

JORDAN Yeah, but two trumpets, no piano? (*In awe*) How you guys played those changes with just a *bass* comping. I don't think I—

DANIEL (*Not wanting to get sucked in*) I don't remember. Look at this place. The pipes. The wires. From the ceiling! It's like a Booth cartoon. Or Bosch. What happened to the kitchen? You know, Martha used to be able to cook in there.

JORDAN (*Stuffing bag with provisions*) Not anymore. He's mostly take-out. And Diet Pepsi. Chewable Vitamin C's—although he says they're hard on the kidneys. And cigarettes. Since the coma he's switched to those organic Indian ones. He's decided it's the additives in cigarettes that do you in.

DANIEL (*Walking toward offstage kitchen*) It's like the twentieth century never happened. Marty was always a Luddite. You know, he never even learned how to drive. I mean—oh my God!

JORDAN What?

DANIEL That sink. There's all this . . . stuff at the bottom.

JORDAN Probably Chinese food. Hundred-day-old egg foo yung . . . I'll take care of that.

DANIEL Where's the switch for the disposal?

JORDAN Um—disposal?

DANIEL Isn't there a—

JORDAN Ohhh . . . *No one* in New York has those. In fact, I think yours was the first one I ever—

DANIEL Mine? At the condo, you mean? . . . I take it Delia hasn't seen your place.

JORDAN I'm working up to it, slowly—very slowly. I'm in the Bronx. You remember the Bronx. I want her to fall for me, not for the glamour.

DANIEL Look, Jordan. For all I know you might be a good kid. But let's face reality here—you are not in Chuck's league.

JORDAN (*No idea who Chuck is*)   Sorry?

DANIEL   You know what they used to call your father? The relief band. Second chair. I'll wait downstairs in the car.

SCENE FOUR

Martin, alone in the condo. He has been given a tripodlike cane, which he has no idea how to use. He is winded. And also overwhelmed by the apartment. He's trying to figure out how to get the stereo volume down. But the remote control doesn't work. Or it turns on the TV. Or changes the station on the tuner. Now he looks up to see Daniel has let himself in.

DANIEL   YOU'RE HERE?

MARTIN   WHAT?

DANIEL   TURN THE VOLUME—

MARTIN   NOTHING WORKS IN THIS FUCKING—

DANIEL   YOU'VE GOT THE—

Martin drives Daniel crazy with his inability to figure out the remote. Daniel takes it away from him, hits a few buttons . . .

MARTIN   THEY SHOULD JUST HAVE A . . .

And order is restored.

MARTIN (*cont.*)   . . . KNOB.

DANIEL (*Exhales*)   When did you get here?

MARTIN   A couple of hours ago. The hospital was so gassed to see me go, they popped for an ambulette. And a twenty-one-syringe salute.

Daniel looks at a take-out mess on the normally pristine coffee table.
Starts to clean up.

DANIEL Made yourself at home, I see—

MARTIN You want some? Lo mein.

DANIEL Listen, Martin—I know it seems like no one lives
here. And the place is pretty comfortable, but you do
understand this is only temporary. Very tem—

MARTIN I hope to God it's only temporary.

DANIEL What—

MARTIN I can't figure out how anything works in this friggin'
place. The sink, no faucets, just like a silver gooseneck in
the middle. A tiller of some sort. And the drain has this
thing in it, the fork falls in, I hit the switch and it's like
Vesuvius, in reverse. I almost lost my fucking hand. Here's
your fork, by the way.

Martin hands Daniel a mangled fork.

DANIEL You have to be—

MARTIN I can't figure out how to turn on any of the fucking
lights—I can't even open a window.

DANIEL That's because they're sealed, Martin.

MARTIN Sealed?

DANIEL Sealed. Sealed. We're thirty floors up, the city's filthy,
it's loud. Why would *anyone* want to open a window? Use
the DēLonghi!

MARTIN The what—

Daniel points to an unseen heating/cooling unit.

DANIEL The De—Toward the red is hot; toward the blue is cold, like in the bathroom.

MARTIN Yeah, where there's also no faucets—just strange little bottles of vowel-free shampoos. And a black toilet. What is *that* about? How much does this place cost you?

DANIEL A little over five hundred.

MARTIN You got this for five bills a month, Danny? That's a steal. My place is up to 390 if you can believe that.

DANIEL This is a condo, Martin. I, we—the corporation owns it. We bought it. For a little over five hundred thousand dollars. And, yes, it *was* a steal.

MARTIN You're shittin' me. Five hundred grand. And I couldn't turn the water off? I had the kid come up, he shut everything down.

DANIEL The kid?

MARTIN At the door, nice kid, Dominican I think.

DANIEL Is he.

MARTIN He told me his mother's been sick too—with cancer. I said, "That's tough." And he says, "This is it. We come and we go."

DANIEL (*Not listening*) *Now, about the answering machine*—I don't want—I can't have you putting your name on the—it's a business phone. Just turn the volume up; if it's for you, from us, pick up.

MARTIN You can tell Martha I said she did a nice job decorating. I never knew there were so many shades of black.

DANIEL I'm not telling Martha anything. No one is. When you're out of here we'll send in a small brigade to clean up and wash down—

MARTIN —and fumigate?

DANIEL —and she will never know.

MARTIN She hates me that much?

DANIEL We don't talk about you.

MARTIN Did you tell her I'm clean now? I haven't . . . in years.

DANIEL Martin, it has nothing to do with that.

MARTIN I mean you were the one who got me hooked. I don't see why she—

DANIEL It has nothing to with that.

MARTIN Bullshit. She blamed me. Everything she hated about you, she pinned on me: the booze, the dope—

DANIEL She saved my life. I wouldn't be—I'd be dead if it weren't for her. If I'd gone back for you, we both would have drowned.

MARTIN You think you didn't drown.

DANIEL I gave up a lot . . . But I have done all right for myself, Martin . . . I've a home, a business, a family.

MARTIN "Richard Cory, one calm summer night—"

DANIEL (*Pointedly*) I am not alone.

MARTIN "—Went home and put a bullet through his head."

DANIEL Oh, that's right! You always were the "smart one." The shit-out-of-luck con man with "a heart of gold."

63

MARTIN Con *artist.*

DANIEL Bullshit! You're a career junkie. You've never taken responsibility for anyone or anything. Not even your music!

MARTIN How would you know? You aced me out. I'm your twin, I'm blood, and I don't fucking exist. You let Martha airbrush me out. She purged me and you never said a word.

DANIEL That's right, blame me—

MARTIN All because—

DANIEL —for everything that's gone wrong in your life—

MARTIN All because I walked in on her and Eddie.

DANIEL What?

MARTIN She never forgave me, and you never—

DANIEL Eddie? Eddie? You poor bastard . . . It's not Eddie. It's . . . the kid.

MARTIN Delia? She came out fine. I'm hardly going to undo twenty-five years of . . . of hydroponic child rearing.

DANIEL I'm not talking about Delia, Martin.

MARTIN What?

DANIEL The first one.

It takes Martin a while to understand the reference.

MARTIN Jesus.

DANIEL It took us ten years to get over it.

MARTIN So. What did I have to do with that?

DANIEL You know Martha—

MARTIN All I was was your answering service.

DANIEL She gets an idea in her head and—

MARTIN —she thinks I never gave you *that* message?

DANIEL Marty—by the time I came home, both of us— Martha and I—we were so strung out . . . I couldn't—

MARTIN —tell her the truth. Could you?

DANIEL (*Completely shaken now*) I don't think it's ever come up.

SCENE FIVE

Jordan and Delia in a subdued, upscale restaurant.

JORDAN What do you mean, it never came up?

DELIA I don't know.

JORDAN Did you just forget you were engaged?

DELIA I didn't think it was relevant.

JORDAN Come again?

DELIA I thought—At first, I didn't think we'd go out. It never crossed my mind.

JORDAN Thank you.

DELIA And then we started to go out, I just didn't think—we never defined what we, you know . . . So I—

JORDAN You didn't think you needed to tell me you were engaged.

DELIA I figured why have a . . . confrontation for no reason? Chuck wasn't due back till fall—

JORDAN And we'd probably be played out by then?

DELIA It wasn't clear—

JORDAN It would've been a lot more clear if you wore a ring.

DELIA It's being cut.

JORDAN What does Chuck know?

DELIA He's in Hong Kong. Working twenty-hour days—this is a major buyout—you have no idea how all-consuming these takeovers can be. He's under a lot of stress and I'm not—

JORDAN AND I'M NOT. HELLO? Martin was in a coma. He listed me as his next of kin. His health care's running out.

DELIA Don't shout, we're in a restaurant.

JORDAN Is that why we're in a restaurant? So I WON'T SHOUT?

DELIA Jordan, please. I didn't mean to hurt you.

JORDAN What does intent have to do with it?

DELIA I didn't mean to—I just figured, Chuck was away, I didn't know when he was coming back. I was enjoying your company but, I mean, we could not be from more—

JORDAN So you were deigning to slum with me for a few months, and you figured, when it was over I'd be grateful for the notch on my Gucci belt.

DELIA (*Reflexively*) It's a Coach.

JORDAN What?

DELIA (*Now with no choice but to explain*)   It's a Coach belt, not a Gucci. Gucci is gauche.

JORDAN   You're a piece of work, Delia. A real piece of work.

DELIA   I'm sorry Jordan.

He doesn't say anything.

DELIA (*cont.*)   I'm really quite fond of you.

JORDAN   You are?

She nods. She's genuinely sad now.

JORDAN (*cont.*)   So why can't we—

DELIA   Jordan, I can't. I'm just—Chuck is—He's the boy next door. I've known him since I was a kid. We used to call him the Golden Retriever. Our families skied together, every Christmas, Gstaad—we're almost like brother and sister.

JORDAN   Do you hear yourself?

DELIA   We're a good team.

JORDAN   What are we—

DELIA   I don't know.

JORDAN   —a good last fling?

DELIA   Jordan. I'm almost twenty-six. I want to settle down. I want to have the kind of marriage my parents have.

JORDAN   There's a role model.

DELIA   What does that mean?

JORDAN   Look, I'm done being your tour guide.

Jordan slams some money on the table, leaves.

DELIA Jordan—

JORDAN Ask your father.

DELIA —wait!

JORDAN What?

She catches up to him, he turns to her, they begin to make out furiously in a stairwell.

SCENE SIX

Then they separate. Delia goes to Martin's condo. Martin looks at her. She's a wreck.

MARTIN What happened to you?

DELIA Jordan and I had . . . sex in the stairwell.

MARTIN Ohhh . . . you're breaking up with him.

DELIA Why would you think that?

MARTIN A girl like you doesn't have sex in the stairwell with someone she knows, unless she also knows she's never going to see him again.

DELIA A "girl like me"? How would you—

MARTIN You didn't dump him?

DELIA Can I . . . have a drink.

MARTIN Help yourself . . . there's miniscotch, minibourbon, Minnie Minoso . . . (*Sees no point in explaining this*) never mind.

DELIA It was never going to work with me and—he's from Mars, I'm from—

MARTIN Greenwich.

She takes a long sip of her drink.

DELIA Daniel told him I'm engaged.

MARTIN And are you?

DELIA If I say yes, will you hate me?

MARTIN (*Surprised by her double life*) Oh boy . . . you are your mother's little girl.

DELIA What does that mean?

MARTIN Ask your mother.

DELIA She's away.

MARTIN Still? Then ask your father.

DELIA Martin, please. You're the only one who'll be straight with me.

MARTIN That's not a good sign.

DELIA They kept you away from me my whole life—what were they afraid of?

MARTIN Beats me.

DELIA Come on. All of these secrets, just to—I'm not stupid. It doesn't add up. You know it doesn't.

MARTIN No. (*After long pause*) What did the toupee maker say after the burglary?

DELIA Martin—

MARTIN There's a piece missing here . . .

Your father and I were touring—'55, '56. The album had come out—*Brothers in Swing*—and we had bookings. Scattered everywhere. Your mother was back in New York. And she was . . . pregnant. Very pregnant. It's a bad winter. And she's there—in the walk-up—alone. Sophie, the super's wife, was checking in on her. And every other night, after a gig, if I pestered him enough, Danny would call from a pay phone, reversing the charges. But mostly he's . . . out. And sometimes your mother'd call the motel late, and I'd pretend he was passed out, or in the john. The next day he'd tell her I forgot to give him the message. Brother stuff.

Then one night, coldest night of the year in New York, she calls. We had just closed in L.A., she calls at like, 5 A.M. She's hemorrhaging.

DELIA Oh no . . .

MARTIN She takes herself to the emergency room—loses the kid.

DELIA Oh, God . . .

MARTIN It was a boy. Miscarriage. Something. And of course, I don't see your father, for like two days. He's just—out. And she's calling. And I don't know what to tell her. And she is flipping out at me. Finally Danny shows up in . . . San Francisco, ten minutes before the gig starts. And, you'll pardon me, but he's stoned out of his mind. Planets away. And I tell him what happened. And he looks at me and says, "Probably wasn't my kid anyway."

Then he goes up on the bandstand and he plays his ass off. Way, way, way over his head. Four straight hours. The drummer's hands are bleeding. Danny's the reincarnation of Fats Navarro and Bix Beiderbecke rolled into one. He plays out the week like a kamikaze. By the end of the gig, he's a zombie, and the record companies are all over him.

Then he goes home. And that was that.

As far as I know, he never touched the horn again.

Martha finds him passed out in the stairwell. Goes nuts on him. He comes to and says, "I had no idea, Marty never told me."

DELIA (*Exhaling*) Oh my God.

MARTIN Martha spent the next three months cradling his head while he sweats it out. Cold turkey. She buried the kid. He buried me. That was their—it was the only way they could go on.

Delia has been trying to process the story; she is overwhelmed.

DELIA Oh God. Oh God. Oh God.

MARTIN Delia, I—

DELIA What did my dad mean by, "It probably wasn't my kid anyway"?

MARTIN Who knows?

DELIA Martin—

MARTIN He thought it was Eddie's. I guess.

DELIA Was it?

MARTIN Fielder's choice, the way I heard it.

DELIA That would have made the baby Jordan's—

MARTIN Delia—

DELIA Which would make Jordan, what . . .

Delia is reeling, from everything.

71

MARTIN Hey—leave it be. Eddie married Jordan's mom, God help her. Martha married Dan. *You guys* were born years later. Like Macy's and Gimbel's, close . . .

DELIA But no relation.

SCENE SEVEN

Jordan enters the condo with a supermarket bag. He sees Martin, who has chain-smoked but otherwise not moved since the last scene. His health is clearly getting worse again.

JORDAN Martin—I brought you some Diet Pepsis. And a diabetic cake. And some cholesterol-free single-malt scotch.

MARTIN How thoughtless, put her there.

JORDAN Happy birthday, old man.

He pats him.

MARTIN You look lousy.

Jordan pours them both a scotch.

JORDAN So: She doesn't call for three weeks, then she finally calls and lets slip that her . . . fiancé—

MARTIN Some guy named Merrill Lynch?

JORDAN *Chuck,* is back.

Martin offers a toast.

MARTIN Ashes to ashes, trusts to trusts.

JORDAN He's taking her antiquing. I'm bleeding in the gutter, and she's sipping her chardonnay.

MARTIN Hey, Jordy, you weren't going to marry her.

JORDAN Who knows?

MARTIN "Rich girls don't marry poor boys," Gatsby.

JORDAN She has no idea she's done anything wrong. You were right, the acorn does not fall far from the tree . . .

MARTIN *Jordy*—

JORDAN I mean, nothing gets to her. Nothing. Son of Sam had more guilt.

MARTIN Hey, Jordan! I think you may be . . . a little over the top here. I mean, even Greenwich girls are entitled to one last tune-up.

JORDAN What?

MARTIN Right before they marry is classic, you'll be happy to know. Dickie Smith had a friend, a printer—wedding invitations: The guy made out *like a bandit.*

JORDAN You are a font, Martin, a never-ending font.

MARTIN Like I always say, "those who can't screw, preach."

JORDAN Is everything a joke to you Martin? Jesus, enough.

Jordan pours himself a drink.

MARTIN Sorry Jordan. I don't mean to be a bore.

JORDAN Why stop now?

MARTIN But I have been down this road . . . I spent thirty-five years with my head buried in the score: Danny's a sellout. Martha wishes me dead.

JORDAN And I've spent the last fifteen years feeling sorry for you—

MARTIN Me too, and the other day—

JORDAN   The least you could do—

MARTIN   —I finally look up—

JORDAN   —is return the favor once before you—

MARTIN   —*I finally look up,* and I'm thinking, maybe an eighth note has gone by—

JORDAN   Martin—

MARTIN   —and instead it's my life. (*After a pause*) And you want to know the beauty part? As long as I could scapegoat them, I never once had to look in the mirror.

Jordan looks at him.

A beat. Now Delia comes in, loaded down with two huge shopping bags.

DELIA   Oh, hello.

MARTIN   Delia.

DELIA (*To Jordan*)   Am I interrupting?

Jordan doesn't say anything.

MARTIN (*To Jordan*)   You remember my niece.

JORDAN   Hi.

DELIA (*Nervous*)   How are you? I mean, hello.

JORDAN   I should be going.

MARTIN (*À la Groucho*)   Hello I must be going—

DELIA   No, I'm sorry, I can't really stay. You—

JORDAN   Groucho Marx.

DELIA   What?

JORDAN   He's doing Groucho.

MARTIN   The comedian, not his brother, the department store.

DELIA (*Figures out the punch line*)   Spencer. Marks and Spencer?

JORDAN   London store.

JORDAN & **DELIA**   No relation.

MARTIN   You two are made for each other.

JORDAN   Want to stay for the party?

DELIA   I'm meeting Chuck, and his folks, for dinner.

JORDAN   I bet he doesn't complain about the bill.

MARTIN   Play nice, Jordan.

JORDAN   Sorry. Anyone for macadamia nuts?

He gets up, takes the cake, goes to the kitchen. She waits a moment.

DELIA   I really can't stay. I just . . . I got you something.

MARTIN   Why? (*Loud, for Jordan*) Because I'm on Jordan's side?

DELIA   Today is Daniel's birthday.

MARTIN   So it is.

DELIA   And I realized, that means it's also your birthday.

MARTIN   Actually, my birthday is six minutes later than Dan's.

DELIA   He says twelve.

MARTIN   Did he? He was always very vain.

DELIA   So, um, here. This one first.

He opens it—stares. Delia pulls another box out of the bag.

DELIA   This is a Walkman, and *this* is a Discman. They're both portable. One for tapes, one for CDs—for when you go to the physical therapy place.

MARTIN   I'm not going to physical therapy. I'm not going to wear a sweatshirt with stains on it, or those god-awful bumblebee sneakers.

She puts a big box in front of him.

MARTIN (*cont.*)   Delia—

DELIA   It's a minicomponent system. For when you go back to Yorkville. It's got a remote control and, um, double cassette so you can make tapes for your friends. Jordan says you like to do that—Oh and here's some CDs, because Jordan says you have, you mostly have records. Is that possible?

She pulls out dozens of CDs, as Jordan reenters with three slices of cake. Martin's has an upturned, lit cigarette in it.

MARTIN   What did you do—roll Sam Goody?

DELIA   Sorry?

JORDAN   He means rob a record store. (*Re: the cake*) I couldn't find any candles.

MARTIN   I couldn't blow 'em out, anyway.

The cake is passed around. Delia takes a bite. She tries to hide her distaste for the cake.

JORDAN   It's diabetic.

DELIA   It's good.

She takes another bite. Then, she breaks the increasingly awkward silence.

DELIA (*To Jordan*) Daniel loved his gift—he wanted me to thank you.

JORDAN Did he?

MARTIN You got my brother a gift? Quisling.

JORDAN I just told her where to go.

DELIA A trumpet.

MARTIN You're kidding.

JORDAN What did he say?

DELIA He just looked at it for a while, in the case. Then he picked it up, and . . . he started to cry.

MARTIN If he cried, imagine what Martha did.

DELIA Um—actually, it turns out, this is . . . Mother and I finally talked. She told me she and Daddy—they're having a . . . trial separation.

JORDAN Really.

DELIA She says they've been separated since Nepal. That's why she didn't come home with him.

JORDAN What's she been doing over there?

DELIA She said she has (*To Martin*) an unmourned loss and she's on a spiritual quest.

JORDAN Whatever that means.

MARTIN It means she's fucking her sherpa.

JORDAN (*To Delia*) What does your father say?

DELIA Nothing yet. And it was his birthday, so I—

Martin's cough has turned into a coughing jag. They go to him.

77

DELIA Are you OK?

MARTIN Get me a—(*Coughs*)

JORDAN Cigarette?

MARTIN Water.

JORDAN Water?

Jordan rushes to the minibar for it.

MARTIN What the hell. It's good enough for the fucking fish.

Drinks it. He's shaking. It's a serious attack—his system is shutting down.

DELIA Are you—

MARTIN I'm all right.

JORDAN Martin—

MARTIN (*Pissy*) I said I'm all right.

DELIA I'd better be going, Chuck is, um . . .

JORDAN Spare me the details, thank you.

DELIA (*To Martin*) OK if I check in on you, Uncle Martin?

MARTIN OK if I check out on you?

The two hold, then hug each other. Now she walks to the door, where Jordan has been waiting.

DELIA So long, Jordan. You gonna be OK?

JORDAN Me? No.

DELIA Me neither.

JORDAN Good-bye.

He starts to offer a polite hug. She kisses him. On the lips,
passionately. He responds, and she pulls away. Leaves. Jordan looks
back to Martin, who watched the whole good-bye, but now turns away.

JORDAN She kissed me. What the hell is that?

MARTIN Confusion.

JORDAN I'll say.

MARTIN Martha left Dan? Can you believe that? After thirty-
five years. The Berlin Wall, the Soviet bloc, and now,
Martha . . .

He fights back his cough . . .

JORDAN Listen, I'm sorry I didn't do more of a—you know,
"Happy Birthday" thing. I've—

MARTIN Jordan, this was one of the nicest birthdays I've had.

JORDAN Uh-huh. Next year I'll—

Martin touches Jordan, paternally.

MARTIN I'm not kidding, Jordy. Thank you . . . for
everything.

Scene Eight

Music up: Two trumpets, unaccompanied, play a slow sweet blues.
Daniel, alone in Connecticut, listens, with a new trumpet in his
hands. He waits for the phone call he's made to connect.

In New York, Martin, exhausted, sits on the couch. He lets the
answering machine pick up. After the beep:

DANIEL Marty, it's your brother, if you'll pardon the
expression. Pick up. . . . Marty? It's Danny.

Martin doesn't pick up the phone. He listens to Dan's message.
(Note: An actual phone is not neccesary for Dan.)

DANIEL   Oh well. I got a little time on my hands up here now.
So I'm rummaging in the attic, and I find these old rehearsal
tapes—warm-ups, warm-downs—from the B-Sharp opening,
1953–54. I had no idea I had the stuff. Those were sweet days
. . . Don't stop me if you've heard the story.

I'll send you a tape. Ah, you probably have it. Oh—dig
this: Delia, ah, (*Gets a little choked up*) she got me a horn.
For my birthday. Our birthday. Actually. And I didn't
think, I mean, it's been almost thirty-five years, I didn't
think I could get a note out of the damn thing, but ah—I
started noodling. Gently. Very gently. And you're not going
to believe this, but I got up to a G. You know, a middle
one, but still.

So, ah, anyway. Since I have some time all of a sudden I
was thinking maybe to come into the city . . . I'll take the
train. Hey, remember in Frisco that time when Lawrence
Welk introduced the song, "Now, ladies and gentlemen,
we're going to play Duke Ellington's '*Take* a Train'"?

The brothers shrug their shoulders in unison.

DANIEL (*cont.*)   I think it was Frisco. Where was I? Oh—I'll
come in and you and I could, you know . . . listen to the
tapes.

*Now Martin slowly gets his bag and tape player. Slowly, painfully,
walks to the door. Short of breath.*

*Martin and Daniel cross each other onstage. Martin struggling to get
back to his walk-up, Dan pacing his home.*

DANIEL (*cont.*)   Or maybe even go hear Jordan's band. Or you
know, whatever. Do you think he'd mind if I came? I bet
he can play. OK . . . Give me a blast, when you get the

chance, Marty. And, ah—Happy Birthday. Belated . . . Good-bye Marty.

The two brothers listen to the same tape, separately. Now, as it ends, Martin stands straight, he and Danny share a look, then he starts to walk off, free.

As he and Danny exit, Jordan enters. Glimmmer, Glimmer and Shine listen for the briefest of moments.

Scene Nine

Just following the brothers' exits, Delia enters. She sees Jordan. Both can barely hold it together.

DELIA   How did it happen?

JORDAN   He wasn't at the condo, so I tried his place, and I found him on the sofa, with your headphones on.

DELIA   That's . . . How did he even *get*—?

JORDAN   The doorman at your place told me he just said, "Time to go." He took a few bags. I don't know how he climbed up the stairs.

DELIA   Why couldn't he just stay put—

JORDAN   He's stubborn. I think maybe he wanted to go home, to . . .

DELIA   I'm so sorry, Jordan . . . I—

JORDAN   I found this—with your name on it.

He hands her a manila envelope. She opens it.

DELIA   It's that photo, of, um—he wrote something on the back. (*Reading*) "To my dearest niece, and—"

81

JORDAN   He's a bit floral sometimes.

DELIA (*Reading*)   "To my dearest niece, and Jordan,
This is a photo I saved from 1955, which Martha never
forgave me for. It's Delia's mother, of course, and Jordan's
father, when they were both young, and very much in love
. . . and too dumb to say it.
I for one, am grateful to them; for had they not blown it,
they would not have settled into the lives they led, and I
would never have met you both.
"Never settle,
Martin."

Delia turns to Jordan, as the lights fade.

END OF PLAY